AI for Anyone: The Beginner's Guide to AI

By Sebastian Huelswitt

Table of Contents

Foreword

My foray into writing, specifically on the topic of AI, stems from the fact that I had many of the same questions which this book hopes to answer not too long ago. The world is changing, and this step change in AI has prompted what I believe will be the second iteration of the 4th industrial revolution.

This book's only focus is to bring someone to the first step of the AI journey. As such, I've kept the language as jargon-free and as simple as possible. I hope this guide helps people go from zero involvement with AI to a point at which they can use AI to help them find the next steps.

I'd also like to highlight the fact that AI was used in the crafting of this book. It was used as an assistant, a guide, and an expert voice to help flesh out the ideas this book is trying to convey. The title page was also created using AI tools.

Introduction: Welcome to Your AI Journey (No Tech Jargon Required!)

Have you felt a bit like you're standing on the sidelines as the world buzzes about **AI**? Perhaps you've been amazed by what computers can do now, like writing entire articles or conjuring up incredible images, and thought, "That sounds amazing, but where do I even *start*? Is it too complicated for me? Will I just get frustrated trying to figure it out?"

If any of that sounds familiar, then you're exactly who this book was written for. Consider this your **AI Compass**, designed specifically for everyday people who might not be tech experts but are curious, ambitious, and ready to explore the incredible potential of artificial intelligence.

Your AI Compass: Why This Book Was Written Just for You

I know from firsthand experience of hearing of this revolution but not knowing what to do with it! We know the common hurdles that can make getting started with new technology feel daunting. It often begins with the confusion of simply **getting started** and figuring out **where to go online** to find these AI tools. Then, once you're in, there's the frustration of trying to "speak" AI's strange language when you're **prompting** it to do something. I've heard it time and time again how people feel overwhelmed by how fast things change in the tech world, making you uncertain if you can truly **trust** what AI generates or how to verify its output. You're likely wondering how these tools can actually help in your **everyday life**, whether for personal projects or more structured tasks, not just in some advanced tech lab. As AI becomes more common, the lines between using it for fun versus for serious **professional tasks** can feel very blurry, leaving you wondering about ethical use and data privacy.

This book tackles all of those real-world frustrations head-on. We'll cut through the jargon, simplify the concepts, and give you clear, actionable steps that you can follow at your own pace. Forget the myths about AI being only for coders or requiring a computer science degree. We'll show you that AI *really* is for the everyday user – a powerful, user-friendly tool that can understand your natural language, not a complex machine that demands you learn its intricate inner workings. Our goal is to empower you to feel confident and capable in this exciting new digital landscape.

A Brief Peek at AI's Journey: From Sci-Fi to Your Screen & What's Out There

You might think AI is a brand-new invention that just popped up, but the idea of intelligent machines has actually been around in books, movies, and even ancient myths for centuries! What's truly new is that these ideas are now becoming part of our daily lives, thanks to massive leaps in computer power and clever programming over the past few decades. The AI you're hearing about today isn't a futuristic robot walking among us, but rather specialised software that can perform tasks that once only humans could do.

Today, AI isn't just one single thing; it's a family of tools, each with its own special abilities. When people talk about AI, they're often referring to **"Chatbots"** like **ChatGPT**,

Gemini, and **Bard**. Think of these as super-smart conversation partners that you can type to. They're excellent at understanding your written questions and responding with their own written words. They can write emails, brainstorm ideas, summarise long documents, explain complex topics, or even tell you a story. If you need words, ideas, or information, these are your primary companions. Then there are "**Image Generators**" like **Midjourney** and **DALL-E**. These are the tools that take your written descriptions and magically conjure up incredible pictures and artwork that never existed before. You simply type what you imagine – a "dragon flying over a futuristic city," or "a cosy café on a rainy day, impressionist style" – and they bring it to visual life. They're perfect when you need a unique image for a project, a presentation, or just for fun.

This book will focus on mastering these most popular and accessible types – the text and image generators – giving you practical skills you can use right away. You'll learn how to approach each one for the best results, transforming your ideas into tangible text and visuals.

The Power of Practical AI: What You'll Unlock

With this guide, you're going to discover the immense **Power of Practical AI** that fits seamlessly into your daily life. It's not about becoming a tech guru; it's about making your life easier and more interesting. Imagine **boosting your productivity** in ways you might not have thought possible. You could draft emails that are just right, summarise long articles in a flash, or organise your thoughts and plans for a project in minutes, freeing up valuable time for other activities. You'll also learn how to **unleash your**

creativity in exciting new ways. Whether you're brainstorming fresh ideas for your hobbies, crafting unique images for personal projects like invitations or scrapbooks, or even getting help to write that story, poem, or song you've always dreamed of creating, AI can be your muse and collaborator. Ultimately, you'll be **navigating the digital frontier with confidence**. You'll no longer feel left behind by new technology. Instead, you'll feel empowered by it, understanding how to harness its capabilities to enhance your daily routines and tackle challenges with greater ease.

This isn't about becoming an AI programmer or a data scientist; it's about becoming a master of asking AI the right questions – a "prompt engineer" – to get the results *you* want, effortlessly and on your own terms.

Your Roadmap to Mastery: How This Guide Will Transform Your Experience

This book is your step-by-step **roadmap to mastery**. We'll walk you through everything, starting from that very first login. We'll demystify the process of crafting clear, effective prompts that make AI truly "listen" to your intentions. You'll then explore practical applications for both your personal life and, with careful consideration, your professional tasks. We'll also show you proven strategies to troubleshoot when things don't go as planned, and most importantly, teach you how to use AI safely and ethically, ensuring your privacy and producing reliable results.

By the end of this guide, you won't just understand what AI is; you'll be actively using it confidently and effectively. You'll unlock a whole new level of possibility for your everyday life and creative endeavours, ready to embrace the future with a powerful new skill set. Let's get started on this exciting journey together!

Chapter 1: Stepping into the AI World – Your Zero-Stress Setup

Remember that feeling of excitement mixed with a tiny bit of worry about trying something new online? Perhaps it was setting up your first email account, joining a new social media site, or even downloading a new app on your smartphone. Getting started with AI can feel a lot like that. But here's the good news: just like you mastered those other tools, you can absolutely master AI. This chapter is your welcoming committee, guiding you past those initial "where do I even begin?" moments, so you can step into the AI world with zero stress and a clear path forward.

1.1 Your First AI Doorstep: Choosing & Accessing the Right Tools

The first big question many people have is, "Which AI should I even use?" It can feel like there are a million new names popping up every day, all with slightly different purposes. Don't worry, we're going to keep it simple to start, focusing on the two main types you'll likely encounter first, and guiding you on where and how to find them.

ChatGPT, Gemini & Bard: Your Conversational AI Companions. Think of these as incredibly smart assistants you can chat with, almost like a very knowledgeable friend who's always available. They're fantastic for anything involving words and ideas – writing, brainstorming, summarising long documents, explaining complex topics, or even helping you plan. You interact with them by typing in a chat window, much like you would in a text message conversation or an instant messenger. If your primary goal is to generate text – whether it's drafting a polite email to a neighbour, creating a list of imaginative gift ideas, getting a concise summary of a lengthy news article, or even outlining the plot for a short story you're thinking of writing – these are your absolute go-to tools. They excel at understanding your written instructions and responding with their own beautifully crafted written words. Imagine having a super-fast researcher, a talented writer, and a tireless idea generator all rolled into one, available right there in your web browser. They're perfect when you need words, facts (which you'll learn to verify!), or creative ideas quickly and efficiently.

Midjourney & DALL-E: Unleashing Your Inner Visual Artist. These are the awe-inspiring tools that take your written descriptions and magically conjure up incredible, unique pictures and artwork that have never existed before. You simply type what you imagine – maybe "a serene garden with a bubbling fountain, in the style of an oil painting," or "a futuristic city skyline at sunset, photorealistic" – and they bring it to visual life. When your project or idea needs a visual element, these are the tools for you. Perhaps you need a custom image for a presentation at your club, a unique illustration for a homemade birthday card, a distinct background for a family photo album, or even just want to see a wild, creative idea come to life visually. They interpret your descriptions and use powerful AI to "draw" or "paint" a brand new image. They're ideal when you need a unique visual flair without needing to pick up a paintbrush, learn complex graphic design software, or spend hours searching for the perfect stock photo.

So, the choice of tool really boils down to **what you want to create or achieve.** If it's words, ideas, or information you need to process or generate, you'll naturally lean towards the conversational AI tools. If it's a stunning visual, a piece of art, or a unique graphic, the image generators are your best bet. Sometimes, you might even use both in tandem: for instance, using a chatbot to brainstorm detailed ideas for a new painting, and then using an image generator to create visual mock-ups based on those ideas. For most of these tools, you'll simply visit their **official website** through your internet browser. There's no complicated software to download and install onto your computer, at least not for getting started, which keeps things simple and stress-free. We'll guide you directly to the right online destinations, ensuring you land exactly where you need to be to begin your AI journey.

1.2 The Gentle Login: Navigating Accounts & Security

Once you've decided which AI tool you want to try, the very next step is almost always creating an account. If you've ever signed up for online banking, a shopping website, or a social media profile, you already know most of what to expect! It's a standard process designed to keep your interactions private and secure.

You'll typically look for clear buttons or links that say something like "Sign Up," "Get Started," "Create Account," or "Try Free." Clicking one of these will lead you to a form where you'll usually need to provide a valid email address. This email will be your primary way to access your account and receive any important notifications. After entering your email, you'll be prompted to choose a password. This is a crucial step! Remember to pick a **strong, unique password** – ideally one you don't use for any other online service. Combining uppercase and lowercase letters, numbers, and symbols is always a good practice. Many sites will even show you a strength indicator as you type, helping you create a secure password. After you've filled out the initial sign-up form, many AI services, just like banks or social media platforms, will send a verification code to your email address or, sometimes, to your phone number. This is a very common security measure known as "two-factor authentication" or "multi-factor authentication." It might feel like an extra step that slows things down, but it's incredibly important. This process helps the service ensure that you're a real person and not an automated program, and it adds an extra layer of protection to your account against unauthorised access. Simply check your email inbox (or spam folder, just in case!) or your phone's text messages for the code, then enter it into the provided field on the website. Once you've successfully created your account and completed any verification steps, you'll be logged in! It's natural to feel a tiny bit of apprehension, staring at a new screen. However, you'll likely see a surprisingly simple interface. For chatbots, this usually means a large, blank box where you can type your questions or prompts, often with a "Send" button nearby. There might be some introductory messages or quick tutorials, which are always worth a glance. For image generators, the initial screen might be a bit more visual, perhaps showing examples of images or giving you a clear instruction to type your first command. Don't expect flashing lights, complicated controls, or a confusing array of buttons right away. The true power of these tools is often hidden behind their remarkably simple user interfaces, waiting for your words to bring them to life. Just take a deep breath and get ready to type!

1.3 Your Very First AI Exchange: Saying Hello and Seeing the Magic Happen

This is the moment we've been building towards – your first real interaction with an AI! This is where you actually "talk" to the AI, and it talks back (or draws back!). The goal here is just to see it respond, to get a feel for the back-and-forth, and to experience that little spark of "aha!" when your words trigger a reaction.

If you're starting with a chatbot like ChatGPT or Gemini, the screen will typically look quite clean and minimalist. You'll definitely see a clear **prompt box**, usually at the bottom of the screen, where you'll type your questions or instructions. Above that, you'll see the **chat history**, which is essentially a transcript of your conversation as it unfolds. Each time you send a message, it appears here, followed by the AI's response. There might be some small icons or buttons for **settings** or starting a "new chat," but you can safely ignore these for your very first interaction. Focus on the prompt box and the conversation flow. Image generators like Midjourney often have a slightly different interface, sometimes integrating with existing chat platforms like Discord. If you're using Midjourney via Discord, you'll enter specific commands. The most common starting command is usually `/imagine`, followed by your description. It feels a bit like giving very precise instructions to a highly skilled artist who happens to be a robot, which, in a way, is exactly what you're doing! Other image tools might have a single input box on their website where you type your description directly. The key is that your words are the brushstrokes. Let's make your very first prompt incredibly simple. The goal isn't perfection, but connection! For a chatbot, try something friendly and low-stakes: "Hello, what can you do for me?" or "Tell me a fun fact about giraffes." You could also try: "What's a good book for someone who likes historical mysteries?" or "Give me a simple recipe for scrambled eggs." For an image generator, keep your description straightforward: `/imagine a happy golden retriever playing in a park` or `/imagine a quiet beach at sunset, vibrant colours`. Don't overthink it or try to make it perfect right away. The most important part of this step is simply to observe. Seeing that first response, whether it's a few sentences of text or a unique image appearing on your screen, is a little moment of magic. It transforms AI from an abstract concept into a tangible, responsive tool right at your fingertips. You've just begun your journey as an AI creator!

1.4 Chatting vs. Searching: How AI is Different from Google

You're probably very used to "Googling" things when you need information, almost like it's a reflex. So, when people talk about "chatting" with an AI, it's natural to wonder: how is that different from doing a traditional search? It's an excellent question, and understanding the core distinction will help you use both powerful tools much more effectively in your daily life.

Think of Google (or any traditional search engine like Bing or DuckDuckGo) as a super-fast, incredibly comprehensive librarian for the entire internet. When you type in a search query – say, "best hiking trails near me" or "history of the Roman Empire" – Google scans billions of web pages. What it then shows you is a list of *links* to websites, articles, images, and videos where that information already exists. Your job is then to click through those links, read the content, compare different sources, and synthesise the information yourself. It's fantastic for finding existing information, verifying facts, and exploring a wide range of perspectives and sources. You are the active researcher.

AI chatbots, on the other hand, are more like having a direct conversation with a very well-read and articulate assistant who can understand your questions and *generate* a direct answer or new content specifically for you. Instead of giving you a list of links to read, the chatbot processes the information it has learned from its vast training data and synthesises it into a concise, direct response. It can also create entirely new things that don't already exist online, like a draft of an email tailored to your needs, a custom short story, or a brainstorming list based on your criteria. You talk to it, and it talks back, often remembering the flow of your conversation and allowing you to refine your request in real-time.

Knowing when to "chat" and when to "search" will make your digital life much more efficient. Use Google when you need very specific, current, and verifiable facts (like today's weather, a company's exact phone number, the latest news headlines, or specific product reviews). You'd also use it when you want to see multiple perspectives or sources on a topic to form your own opinion, or when you need to find a specific website, product to buy, or service provider. Finally,

Google is ideal when you're looking for images that already exist, like a photo of a famous landmark. Conversely, use AI Chatbots when you need a quick, summarised explanation of a concept without sifting through multiple articles, or when you want to brainstorm ideas, overcome creative blocks, or get help writing original text (like an email, a social media post, or a short script). They're also great if you need help structuring thoughts or breaking down a complex task into simpler steps, or if you want to have a back-and-forth conversation to explore a topic deeply or refine an idea collaboratively. And, of course, use them when you want to generate a brand-new image that doesn't exist anywhere else.

Both are incredibly powerful in their own right, but they serve different purposes. By understanding this distinction, you'll know exactly which tool to reach for, saving you time and getting you the results you need, whether it's information or a creation!

Chapter Summary

Chapter 1: Stepping into the AI World – Your Zero-Stress Setup

- You learned how to **identify and choose** between different AI tools, understanding when to use a chatbot for text or an image generator for visuals.
- You mastered the **simple steps to set up and securely log in** to AI platforms, making your first entry into the AI world stress-free.
- You experienced your **very first successful interaction** with AI, seeing how your words can trigger a response and begin a creative process.
- You now understand the key distinctions between **chatting with AI and traditional online searching**, knowing when each tool is most effective for finding information or generating content.

Chapter 2: Speaking AI's Language – Mastering Basic Prompting

You've taken the first big step: you've opened the door to AI and had a simple interaction. That's fantastic! Now, it's time for the real fun – learning how to "talk" to it so it understands exactly what you need. This might sound a bit tricky, like learning a new language with complicated grammar rules. But think of it more like learning to give really clear, helpful instructions to a very intelligent, but very literal, assistant. This chapter will break down the secrets of **prompting** – the art of crafting your requests – so you can start getting truly useful, and even delightful, results from your AI tools.

2.1 The Clarity Code: Why Your Words Matter to AI

Imagine you're asking a new assistant at home or work, "Could you do that thing for me?" They'd probably look confused, right? They'd need more information: "What 'thing'? For whom? By when? How do you want it done?" AI is exactly the same way. It doesn't guess, it doesn't assume, and it certainly can't read your mind. It relies entirely on the words you give it. This is where "prompting" comes in, and mastering it starts with understanding what we call the "Clarity Code."

Beyond "Tell Me About": The Power of Specificity. When you're searching on Google, you might type "tell me about dogs" and get millions of results. That's fine for broad exploration. But with AI, you can be much, much more precise, and the more specific you are, the better the AI can focus its incredible knowledge on exactly what you want. Instead of saying "Tell me about dogs," which is too vague and might lead the AI to give you a general history or a list of breeds, try something like: "Tell me **five fascinating facts about Border Collies, focusing specifically on their intelligence and their history as herding dogs.**" See the difference? By adding details like "five fascinating facts," "Border Collies," "intelligence," and "herding dogs," you're giving the AI a clear target. It's like having a conversation where you provide explicit, actionable directions instead of vague hints, ensuring the AI delivers a tailored response, not just a generic one.

The Importance of Context: Giving AI the Right Background. Unlike a human who might remember your previous conversations or know your general situation, AI (unless it's within the same continuous chat window) doesn't have a memory. Each new prompt is often a fresh start. So, if you're asking about something specific, it's incredibly helpful to give the AI a little background information, or "context." For example, if you want AI to summarise a recipe, it helps to first say, "Here's a recipe for apple pie: [paste the entire recipe text here]." Then, in a separate, follow-up prompt, you can ask, "Now, summarise *this recipe* in three bullet points, focusing on the key ingredients and steps." You're providing the AI with all the necessary information upfront, making sure it understands exactly what "this recipe" refers to. Without that context, it might try to summarise a generic apple pie recipe from its training data, which might not be the one you're working with.

Defining Your Desired Outcome: What Do You Really Want? Before you even begin typing your prompt, take a moment to pause and think: What *kind* of answer or output do I want? Do you need a simple list of items? A descriptive paragraph? A detailed short story? A professional email to a client? Or, if you're using an image generator, do you want a picture that looks like a realistic photograph, a whimsical watercolour painting, or a stark black-and-white sketch? Instead of vaguely saying "Write about inviting neighbours," try: "Write a **short, friendly email inviting neighbours to a casual potluck this Saturday**, mentioning the time and asking them to bring a dish to share." By clearly telling the AI the *format* (email), *tone* (friendly), and *purpose* (inviting neighbours to a potluck this Saturday), you're setting clear expectations. This greatly influences the AI's response, ensuring it delivers something immediately useful and tailored to your specific needs, rather than a generic piece of writing.

2.2 Your First Successful Prompts: Text & Image Foundations

Now that you understand *why* clarity, context, and defining your outcome matter, let's put these principles into practice with some foundational prompts. These are your essential building blocks, designed to give you a feel for how your words translate into AI actions for both text and image generation. Don't worry about perfection; aim for progress and discovery!

Crafting Effective Chatbot Prompts for Everyday Questions. When interacting with chatbots like ChatGPT or Gemini, remember to start simple, but always be as specific as you can. Think about what you would tell a human assistant if you needed a precise answer or creation. Instead of a vague request like "Ideas for dinner," which is too broad and might lead the AI to give you anything from gourmet recipes to fast-food suggestions, try something like: "Give me **five easy dinner ideas for a family of four using chicken and potatoes**, that can be made in under 30 minutes." Now the AI knows the number of ideas, main ingredients, family size, and time constraint. For creative writing, instead of just saying "Write about my trip" (AI has no idea where or what to focus on), try: "Write a **short, engaging paragraph about my recent trip to the Grand Canyon**, focusing on the **breathtaking views and the feeling of awe** I experienced while standing at the South Rim during sunset." Here, we've added the location, the specific aspect to focus on, and a desired emotional tone.

Building Your First Image Prompt: Key Elements for Visuals. Image generators like Midjourney or DALL-E are like highly artistic robots that rely entirely on your written descriptions. You're effectively telling a painter what to put on their canvas, brushstroke by brushstroke, with your words. Start by identifying the **subject**: What's the main thing you want to see? (e.g., "A cosy cottage"). Then, add **details** about that subject: What specific features does it have? (e.g., "A cosy cottage **with a thatched roof and a smoking chimney**"). Finally, consider the **style** or artistic interpretation: How do you want it to look? (e.g., "A cosy cottage with a thatched roof and a smoking chimney, **watercolour painting style**"). Your first Midjourney prompt, remembering you usually type `/imagine` followed by your description, might be: `/imagine a cosy cottage with a thatched roof and a` `smoking chimney, watercolour painting style`. The AI will then take these words and generate a unique image reflecting your description.

Common Prompting Pitfalls: What NOT to Do (and Why). We all make mistakes when learning something new, and that's perfectly normal! Recognising common pitfalls early on will save you a lot of frustration. The most common mistake is **being too vague**. Asking "Do something cool" or "Make a nice picture" will lead to frustratingly generic, unhelpful results. AI needs guidance; it doesn't intuitively know what "cool" or "nice" means to *you*. It will simply give you a very broad interpretation, which rarely meets your expectations. Another pitfall is **overloading the prompt**. Trying to cram too many unrelated ideas or extremely complex requests into one single sentence can confuse the AI. It's like giving someone ten very different, complicated instructions all at once – they're bound to get lost. If your request is multi-faceted, try to break it down into smaller, sequential prompts within the same chat conversation. Lastly, **assuming prior knowledge** is a common issue. Remember, AI doesn't "know" what you "know" or what you're currently thinking about. If you mention "the project from yesterday" or "that person we discussed," the AI has no idea which project or person you're referring to unless you explicitly remind it or provide the necessary context within the current prompt. Always provide enough information for the AI to understand your current request without relying on assumptions.

2.3 Unlocking Better Results: Keywords and Simple Directives

Once you're comfortable with the very basics of prompting, you can start using specific keywords and simple instructions to make your AI even more effective. These aren't complicated codes; they're just descriptive words that act like fine-tuning dials, allowing you to guide the AI with much greater precision.

For Text: Using Adjectives, Verbs, and Tone Indicators. These words are your secret weapons for guiding AI's writing style and output. Think of them as the specific dials you can turn on a sophisticated machine to fine-tune its performance, helping it understand the precise "flavour" or action you want it to deliver. **Adjectives** are descriptive words that tell the AI *what kind* of text you want. Using words like "**concise**," "**uplifting**," "**detailed**," "**brief**," "**informative**," or "**humorous**" tells the AI about the desired *nature* or *length* of the text. For example: "Write a **concise**, **uplifting** message about starting a new hobby." **Verbs** are action words that directly tell the AI *what to do*. Commands like "**summarise**," "**elaborate**," "**brainstorm**," "**create**," "**explain**," "**compare**," or "**list**" direct its action and the structure of its response. For example: "Now **summarise** this article," "**Elaborate** on this point," "Brainstorm 10 ideas for a retirement party," or "**Explain** quantum physics simply." **Tone Indicators** set the *mood* or *feeling* of the text. Words like "**friendly**," "**professional**," "**humorous**," "**formal**," or "**casual**" ensure the AI's response resonates with your intended audience and purpose. For example: "Write in a **friendly** tone," "Use a **professional** tone for this business proposal," or "Make it **humorous** for a stand-up comedy routine." Combining these elements is powerful: "Brainstorm 5 **creative** and **unique** gift ideas for a gardener who loves exotic plants, written in a **playful** and **enthusiastic** tone." Here, we're combining adjectives for the ideas, and tone indicators for the writing style.

For Images: Adding Style, Lighting, and Subject Details. When you're asking an AI to create a picture, you become the director, the set designer, and the stylist all at once! These elements are your tools for painting a vivid picture in the AI's "mind," ensuring it captures the exact visual you're aiming for. **Style** tells the AI the overall artistic look you want. Do you want it to resemble a "**photorealistic**" image, an "**oil painting**," a "**cartoon**," a "**pixel art**" creation, a "**sci-fi concept art**" piece, a "**charcoal sketch**," or maybe a "**storybook illustration**"? Being specific here is crucial to getting the right artistic feel. **Lighting** dramatically impacts the mood and appearance of an image. Keywords like "**golden hour light**," "**cinematic lighting**," "**moody**," "**bright and airy**," "**dramatic shadows**," or "**soft natural light**" help set the atmosphere of your image. **Subject Details** are the little extras that bring your main subject to life and add richness to the scene. Think about adding phrases like "**intricate details**" for patterns or textures, "**smooth textures**" for a soft feel, "**sharp focus**" for clarity on your main subject, an "**out-of-focus background**" to make your subject stand out, or specifying colours or textures. A combined example would be: `/imagine a majestic lion in a savannah, golden hour light, photorealistic, cinematic shot, with intricate details on its mane.`

A Simple Framework: The "Goal + Context + Detail" Approach. If you're ever feeling stuck or unsure how to structure your prompt, remember this simple recipe. It's a versatile framework that works for almost any AI task, whether text or image. It helps you ensure you're providing the AI with all the necessary ingredients for a successful response. First, state your **Goal**: What do you want the AI to *do*? Be direct. (e.g., "Write a blog post...", "Generate an image of...", "Summarise this information..."). Second, provide **Context**: What background information does the AI need to know to perform the task accurately? (e.g., "...about baking sourdough, assuming the reader is a complete beginner and has never baked bread before...", "...for a website selling artisanal jewellery...", "...from the following historical text..."). Finally, add **Detail**: What specific elements, styles, tones, or formats do you want? This is where you layer on all those adjectives, verbs, tone indicators, and image specifics. (e.g., "...include a list of ingredients, a friendly tone, and keep it under 500 words, highlighting the joy of homemade bread.", "...using a vintage aesthetic with warm colours and soft lighting.", "...in bullet points, focusing on key dates and figures."). This framework will serve you incredibly well as you move to more advanced prompting, giving you a reliable structure for any AI request.

You've just learned the absolute essentials of speaking AI's language! It might seem like a lot of individual pieces at first – understanding clarity, starting with simple prompts, and then adding those powerful keywords like "concise" or "photorealistic." But think of it like learning to drive a car. At first, you focus intently on each individual action: turning the wheel, pressing the pedal, checking the mirrors, signalling. Each step feels separate and requires conscious thought. But soon, with practice, it all becomes second nature, a fluid process where you're intuitively controlling the vehicle.

By applying these basic prompting techniques, you're not just typing words into a box; you're *directing* an incredibly powerful tool. You're giving it the clear, specific instructions it needs to move from providing vague, generic answers to delivering exactly what you're looking for, whether it's a perfectly worded email that sounds just like you, a stunning, unique image that captures your imagination, or a concise summary of a daunting document. This simple yet effective approach is your key to unlocking the true usefulness and magic of AI in your daily life. You're well on your way to becoming a confident AI user and creator, ready to guide your digital assistant with purpose and precision.

Chapter Summary

Chapter 2: Speaking AI's Language – Mastering Basic Prompting

- You grasped the "Clarity Code," learning **why specific, contextualised, and outcome-focused words** are crucial for AI to understand your requests.
- You gained the skill to **craft effective foundational prompts** for both generating text (like emails or ideas) and creating images (by describing subjects and styles).
- You can now **recognise and avoid common prompting pitfalls**, such as being too vague or overloading your requests, ensuring smoother interactions.
- You began to unlock better results by using **descriptive keywords** (adjectives, verbs, tone for text; style, lighting, details for images) and the "Goal + Context + Detail" framework to guide AI.

Chapter 3: Fine-Tuning Your AI – Getting Specific & Nuanced Results

You've taken fantastic strides! In the last chapter, you moved beyond just opening AI tools and learned the basics of "speaking AI's language" to get those first useful results. You're no longer just observing; you're actively interacting and creating! Now, get ready to take your AI skills to the next level. This chapter is all about adding finesse and precision to your instructions, so your AI understands even the trickiest requests and delivers results that are truly specific and tailored to your vision. Think of it as learning to add all the delicate details and perfect shades to a painting, or fine-tuning an instrument until it plays a truly unique and beautiful melody.

3.1 The Art of Iteration: Refining Your AI's Output

You've probably noticed that sometimes your very first prompt, even a well-thought-out one, doesn't get you *exactly* what you wanted. That's perfectly normal – and it's where the real power of AI conversation comes into play! Instead of starting over from scratch when a response isn't quite right, the true magic happens when you engage in a continuous "conversation" with the AI, making small, strategic adjustments to guide it closer and closer to your ideal vision. This process is called **iteration**, and it's a fundamental skill for truly useful AI.

"Make it Better": How to Give Effective Follow-Up Instructions. Don't be afraid to be direct and tell the AI what you didn't like, what it missed, or what could be improved in its last response. Think of it as giving constructive feedback to a diligent but literal assistant. You can use phrases like: "That's a good start, but can you make it sound more encouraging and less formal?" or "The image you generated is nice, but I want the tree in the foreground to be taller and more vibrant." It's important to be specific with your feedback: instead of just "Make it better," try "Make it more concise," "Change the tone to be humorous," or "Add a sense of calm to the image." The AI learns from your feedback within that ongoing conversation thread, remembering what it just produced and what you want to change.

Asking for Alternatives: Getting Multiple Options from AI. Sometimes, you know the general direction you want to go, but you're open to different approaches or creative interpretations. AI is incredibly adept at generating variations based on your prompt, saving you from having to brainstorm them yourself. After an initial response, try asking: "Can you give me three more ideas for that email opening, but each with a slightly different tone?" or "Show me this image again, but with a different artistic lighting style – maybe a sunset glow instead of midday sun?" This technique not only saves you significant time but also often sparks new ideas you might not have considered on your own. It's like having a team of creative minds constantly offering fresh perspectives.

Using Previous Responses: Building on What AI Has Already Generated. Remember from Chapter 2 that AI works best when you give it context. In an ongoing chat, the AI "remembers" the immediate conversation. This means you can build directly on its previous responses, guiding it step-by-step. If the AI has already given you a good piece of text or an image that's close to what you want, you can easily refer back to it. You might say, "Based on the second paragraph you just wrote, can you expand on the idea of community engagement?" or "Using the style and composition of the third image you generated, can you create another one, but this time with a dog instead of a cat?" This helps the AI stay focused on your evolving vision and build upon its own successful work, rather than starting from scratch with each new prompt.

This form of iteration may give you the impression that AI chatbots seem to "remember", and in the immediate ongoing conversation they do. They maintain a continuous context within the specific chat session. However, it's important to understand that the AI itself doesn't have a long-term "memory" of all your past interactions across different sessions or if you close your browser. This brings up an important question: can your work already done be stored and picked up again?

The answer is yes, with a little strategy on your part. When you're using a chatbot, if you close your browser tab, start a new chat, or sometimes even if your session simply times out, the AI's immediate context for *that specific conversation* is typically reset. This means if you start a brand-new chat and ask about "the apple pie recipe," the AI won't know which one you're referring to from a previous session. Similarly, for image generators, while they often keep a history of your generated images within the platform, the AI doesn't inherently remember the *process* you went through or the specific prompt variations you tried unless you manually record them.

To effectively "save" your work and pick it up again, you become your own memory keeper. For text-based AI, the best practice is to **copy and paste** any important conversations, AI-generated drafts (like emails, stories, or outlines), or even the specific prompts that gave you great results, into your own personal document. This could be a simple file on your computer (like a Word document or a Notepad file), a note-taking app (like Google Keep, Evernote, or Apple Notes), or even a dedicated folder in your email. This allows you to re-introduce the context or content to the AI later, by simply pasting it back into the chat window and continuing your instructions. For image-based AI, make sure to **download and save** any images you like, and perhaps keep a record of the exact prompt you used to create them – this way, you can easily replicate or build upon that visual style later.

3.2 Role-Playing & Personas: Guiding AI's Style and Voice

Imagine you need an email written from the perspective of a wise elder, or an image that looks exactly like it was drawn by a specific type of artist. AI can do this incredibly well by "role-playing"! By telling the AI *who* it should pretend to be, or *what style* to adopt, you can dramatically influence the sophistication, tone, and overall feel of its responses, whether they are words or pictures.

"Act as a [Profession/Role]": How to Get AI to Adopt a Role. This is a highly powerful and widely used technique for text generation. You simply start your prompt by explicitly giving the AI a role to assume. For example: "Act as a financial advisor. Explain compound interest in simple terms, using an analogy a beginner can understand." or "Pretend you are a seasoned travel agent. Suggest a 5-day itinerary for a relaxed trip to the Italian countryside, including charming local experiences." The AI will then tap into its vast training data to try its best to respond with the knowledge, tone, vocabulary, and even the presumed "personality" that person would typically use. It's like having a specialist on call for any topic.

Crafting Personas for Text: Tailoring AI's Tone and Persona for Specific Audiences. Beyond specific professions, you can guide the AI to adopt a general "persona" or a particular "tone" that isn't tied to a job title. You might want something "witty and sarcastic," "calm and reassuring," "enthusiastic and energetic," "formal and academic," or "friendly and casual." For instance: "Write a short social media post about my new garden, in a **humorous and slightly self-deprecating tone**." or "Draft a message for my book club, using a **warm and inviting tone** to discuss next month's selection." This ensures the text resonates perfectly with your intended audience, whether they are friends, colleagues, or potential customers.

Influencing Image Style: Directing AI's Artistic Voice. For image generators like Midjourney or DALL-E, you're not assigning a "role" in the same way you would for a chatbot. Instead, you are directly guiding its artistic "voice" or creative approach. You tell it *how* to visualise your idea. You can specify: "**in the style of Van Gogh**," "**a minimalist illustration**," "**like a 1950s comic book**," "**hyperrealistic photography**," "**a fantasy concept art piece**," or even "**an**

abstract digital painting." Adding these artistic style cues tells the AI which visual rules, techniques, and aesthetic principles to follow, giving you much more control over the final visual output and allowing you to achieve diverse artistic effects without any drawing skills yourself.

3.3 Advanced Directives: Constraints, Exclusions, and Precision

Now we're moving into the realm of truly precise prompting, where you can become a meticulous director of your AI. Sometimes, you need the AI to follow very specific rules, include certain elements, or even *avoid* particular things. These advanced directives help you get exactly what you want, eliminating unwanted fluff or problematic elements from the AI's output.

Precision Prompting for Text: Setting Lengths, Formats, and Specific Data Points. You have more control than you think over the structure and length of AI's text responses. You can tell the AI exactly how long something should be or what specific format it should follow. This is incredibly useful for fitting content into specific spaces or for presenting information clearly. For example: "Summarise this article in **exactly 100 words**." "Create a list of pros and cons for working remotely **in bullet points, with a heading for each**." "Write a poem about autumn **with four stanzas, each with four lines, following an AABB rhyme scheme**." Or, "Generate a recipe for chocolate chip cookies, **formatted as a numbered list for ingredients and steps**." This forces the AI to be concise, adhere to a specific structure, and often deliver a more usable output immediately.

Advanced Image Directives: Camera Angles, Moods, and Excluding Unwanted Elements. For images, you can act like a professional film director or photographer, guiding the AI on how to "frame" and "light" the scene you're imagining. Specify **Camera Angles** like "from a **low angle**," "a **wide shot**," "a **close-up portrait**," "an **overhead view**," or "a **dramatic perspective**." This influences how the subject is presented. Describe the emotional atmosphere you want using **Moods**: "serene atmosphere," "chaotic scene," "joyful moment," "mysterious ambiance," or "tense mood." For **Excluding Elements (Negative Prompting)**, sometimes it's easier to tell the AI what *not* to include. In Midjourney, you can use a double dash (`--`) followed by the thing you want to avoid. For instance, `/imagine a beautiful garden --no flowers` would try to generate a garden without any flowers. Other platforms might use "exclude" or "negative prompt" options. This helps you clean up messy results and get rid of elements you definitely don't want, like strange text appearing in an image, or a specific object you don't like.

Layering Prompts: Combining Techniques for Complex Outputs. The real power of advanced prompting comes from cleverly combining all these techniques. You don't have to use them in isolation. You can use role-playing *and* specify a format *and* add a desired tone *and* include a specific lighting style, all within one prompt or across a series of prompts. For text, an example would be: "Act as a personal trainer. Create a 3-day workout plan for a beginner, focusing on home exercises. Use a motivating tone, and present it as a bulleted list with clear instructions for each exercise." For images: `/imagine a medieval` `knight standing before a dragon, epic fantasy art, cinematic lighting, dramatic shadows --no helmet`. This "layering" approach is how you tackle more complex tasks and get highly tailored results that truly match your detailed vision.

3.4 Prompt Troubleshooting: When AI Doesn't Listen (No Tech Required!)

You've tried your best, you've used all the tricks, but sometimes the AI just doesn't seem to "get it." Don't fret! This is where you become a prompt detective, and it's a completely normal part of the process. "Debugging" simply means figuring out why your prompt didn't work as expected and then knowing how to fix it, just like you'd troubleshoot a remote control that isn't working or a coffee maker that's brewing strangely. There's no fancy technical knowledge required, just a bit of patience and a methodical approach.

"Why Isn't It Working?": Demystifying AI Misunderstandings. When AI gives you a strange answer or an image that's completely off, it's usually not being stubborn or faulty; it's simply misunderstood something in your instructions. It's like asking someone for directions and they point you down the wrong street because a key detail was missed or misinterpreted. The problem isn't usually with the AI's capability itself, but with how the instructions (your prompt) were given. AI is literal, so even a tiny bit of ambiguity can send it down the wrong path. Understanding this takes away the frustration and lets you focus on refining your communication with the AI.

Your Simple Checklist: What to Review in a "Stuck" Prompt. If your AI is going off track, pause, take a breath, and review your prompt. This simple checklist can help you pinpoint potential issues. Ask yourself: Is it clear enough? Could a child understand exactly what I'm asking? Are there any vague terms? Is it too vague? Have I used too many general terms (like "good," "nice," "better") instead of specific descriptors? Is it too long or overloaded? Am I trying to cram too many different, unrelated ideas or extremely complex requests into one single prompt? Are there conflicting instructions? Am I telling it to be "short" and "highly detailed" in the same breath, which might confuse it? Did I use the right keywords? Have I included the necessary style words, formats, or specific modifiers that we learned about? Is my context clear? Did I provide all the necessary background information upfront?

The "One Change at a Time" Strategy: Your Step-by-Step Fix. Just like fixing a temperamental light switch or a leaky faucet, when troubleshooting any problem, it's always best to try one solution at a time. This allows you to see exactly what change had an impact. If your prompt isn't working, pick *one* potential issue from your checklist (e.g., "I think it's too vague, I'll make it more specific") and change *only that one thing* in your prompt. Then, try submitting the revised prompt again. If it's still not right, try another single change. This methodical approach helps you quickly pinpoint exactly what's causing the issue and helps you learn what works best for different types of requests.

Ask the AI for Help: When Your Co-Pilot Gets Confused. Here's a clever trick that many experienced AI users employ: sometimes, the AI can even help you debug your own prompt! If you're stuck, you can actually type something like: "I'm trying to get a [type of result, e.g., 'concise summary' or 'detailed image'] about [topic, e.g., 'the history of jazz' or 'a futuristic city'], but it's not working the way I want. Can you suggest how I could rephrase my last prompt for better results?" You're essentially turning the AI into a helpful assistant for *itself* – and for you! It can often identify ambiguities in your previous prompt and offer suggestions for clearer wording, allowing you to learn directly from the tool itself.

You've just completed a pivotal chapter in your AI journey! We moved beyond just asking simple questions and started exploring how to have much more intelligent, precise conversations with your AI tools. You learned that AI isn't a one-and-one machine; it's a dynamic partner you can continuously guide and refine through ongoing dialogue.

We started with the **Art of Iteration**, which is simply the process of making small, smart adjustments to your prompts based on AI's initial responses. This means you now know how to tell AI to "make it better," ask for different options, and even build directly on its previous answers to gradually shape your desired outcome. You then discovered the powerful secret of **Role-Playing & Personas**, learning how to ask AI to adopt a specific voice, tone, or artistic style. This allows it to generate text that sounds like a professional expert or create images that look like they were made by a specific type of artist. Following that, we dived into **Advanced Directives**, showing you how to set precise lengths or formats for text, exclude unwanted elements from images, and combine different instructions for truly complex and tailored outputs.

Perhaps most importantly for your confidence, you gained practical skills in **Prompt Troubleshooting**. No more feeling frustrated or lost when AI misunderstands! You now have a simple checklist to pinpoint what might have gone wrong in your prompt, and effective strategies like the "one change at a time" method to efficiently fix your instructions. You even learned the clever trick of asking the AI itself for help when you're stuck, turning it into your personal "debugging" assistant. All these techniques combine to give you far more control over your AI companion, ensuring it delivers not just *an* answer, but the *right* answer, tailored exactly to your needs. You're no longer just talking to AI; you're expertly directing it to create truly specific, nuanced, and valuable results!

Chapter Summary

Chapter 3: Fine-Tuning Your AI – Getting Specific & Nuanced Results

- You learned the **Art of Iteration**, refining AI's output through ongoing conversation, giving specific feedback, and asking for alternatives to get closer to your ideal.

- You discovered how to **guide AI's style and voice** by using "role-playing" for text (e.g., "Act as a professional") and artistic descriptors for images (e.g., "in the style of Van Gogh").

- You gained control over AI's responses using **advanced directives**, such as setting precise lengths or formats for text, and specifying camera angles or excluding elements for images.

- You acquired practical skills for **troubleshooting prompts**, understanding why AI might misunderstand and how to fix it step-by-step, even asking the AI for help.

Chapter 4: AI as Your Everyday Co-Pilot – Practical Applications

You've mastered the basics of "talking" to AI and even learned how to fine-tune its responses for greater precision. That's fantastic! You've grasped the language of AI, and now it's time to bring AI into your daily routine and truly see how it can become your personal co-pilot. This chapter is all about moving from understanding *how* AI works to actually *using* it in practical, helpful ways for both your daily tasks and your creative projects. Get ready to discover how AI can save you time, spark new ideas, and make everyday life a little easier and more exciting.

4.1 Supercharging Your Productivity: Daily Task Automation

Imagine having a super-efficient, always-available assistant who can tackle those small, often repetitive, and time-consuming tasks that tend to pile up in your day. That's exactly what AI can be for your personal productivity! It's not about replacing what you do, but about streamlining the routine and administrative chores so you have more energy and time for what truly matters to you – whether that's hobbies, family, or more complex thought.

Email Drafting & Response Generation: Saving Precious Time. How many times have you stared at a blank email screen, wondering how to phrase a tricky message just right, or felt overwhelmed by the sheer volume of emails needing a response? AI can be a lifesaver here. You can tell your chatbot: "Draft a polite email declining a meeting invitation for next Tuesday, suggesting an alternative time for late next week," or "Write a quick, professional thank-you email to a colleague for their detailed help with the recent project report." The AI provides a solid, well-structured starting point that you can quickly review and tweak to add your personal touch. This saves you valuable minutes every single day, turning email dread into a quick, manageable task.

Summarising Long Documents & Articles: Grasping Key Info Instantly. Are you faced with a lengthy report for a community group, a detailed news article that's too long to read, or an endless email chain that you need to quickly understand? AI can condense vast amounts of text for you. Simply copy and paste the text into your chatbot and ask: "Summarise this article in three concise bullet points," or "Give me the main ideas from this lengthy document in a short paragraph, focusing on the conclusions." It's like having a lightning-fast reader and editor who can instantly extract the crucial information, allowing you to grasp the core message without getting bogged down in details. This is especially useful for staying informed without spending hours reading.

Efficient Planning: Brainstorming Ideas for Errands, Events, or Projects. Need help organising a birthday dinner, planning a weekend getaway, or breaking down a daunting home improvement project into manageable steps? AI is a fantastic brainstorming and organisational partner. Ask: "Give me a checklist for preparing a small backyard BBQ for 10 people, including food, drinks, and activities," or "Suggest 5 easy, actionable steps for organising my garage this weekend." It can help you think through logistics, anticipate needs, and create actionable plans, turning overwhelming tasks into clear, step-by-step processes.

Organising Information: From Lists to Basic Spreadsheet Data. AI isn't just for generating essays or images; it can be surprisingly good at structuring and organising information. If you have a jumbled list of notes, a collection of ideas, or even raw data that needs a clean format, AI can help. You can ask it to: "Create a shopping list of all the groceries I need for a week of healthy vegetarian eating, categorised by produce, dairy, and pantry items," or "Organise this raw contact data into a simple table with columns for Name, Email, and Phone Number." It takes messy, unstructured information and transforms it into neat, usable formats, whether that's a simple list, a formatted paragraph, or even data ready for a basic spreadsheet.

4.2 Igniting Your Creativity: Beyond the Mundane

AI isn't just a dry, logical machine for crunching numbers or facts; it can be an astonishing source of creative inspiration! If you're a hobbyist, a budding writer, an amateur artist, or just someone who loves exploring new ideas, AI can be your muse, your collaborator, and your personal artistic assistant.

Overcoming Creative Blocks: Brainstorming Ideas for Hobbies, Stories, or Art. Ever stared at a blank page, feeling completely stuck on a story idea? Can't think of a unique craft project for a gift, or a new concept for your painting? AI can be a powerful catalyst to spark your imagination and help you push past creative blocks. Try prompts like: "Give me 10 unexpected plot twists for a mystery novel set in a quiet, seemingly ordinary small town," or "Brainstorm 5 unique ideas for up-cycling old wooden pallets into decorative garden features." It's like having a tireless creative thinking partner who can suggest hundreds of possibilities, helping you find that perfect spark to get started or push an existing project forward.

Crafting Unique Images for Personal Projects: Presentations, Invitations, Crafts. Want a custom image for the background of your family photo album? A unique illustration for a homemade birthday card? Or a cool, original graphic for a presentation at your local club? Image generators are absolutely perfect for this! You can create visuals that are perfectly tailored to your needs and vision, all without needing to be an expert artist or graphic designer. Imagine typing: `/imagine a whimsical garden party invitation, vibrant pastel colours, soft watercolour style, with delicate butterflies and teacups` for a custom event invite. Or, for a more unusual project: `/imagine a serene mountain landscape, created in a pixel art style, suitable for a retro video game background`. These tools empower you to visualise and create exactly what you need, adding a personal and professional touch to any project.

Personalised Learning: Exploring New Topics with AI as Your Tutor. Are you curious about a complex topic but find traditional textbooks or online articles overwhelming? AI can simplify complex subjects and answer your specific questions directly, acting like a personalised tutor. Ask:

"Explain how photosynthesis works in a way a 10-year-old could easily understand, using a garden analogy," or "What are the main theories about why dinosaurs went extinct, explained without scientific jargon?" You can even ask for practice questions, explanations of difficult vocabulary, or step-by-step guides for learning new skills. It's a fantastic, private way to satisfy your curiosity, learn at your own pace, and revisit subjects you've always wanted to understand better.

Fun & Entertainment: Discovering New Recipes, Games, or Travel Ideas. AI can be your go-to for leisure activities too, adding a new dimension to your free time. Need to spice up your weekly meal plan? "Suggest 5 classic board games that are fun for a family game night with teenagers," or "Give me vegetarian dinner recipes that use lentils and are quick to make." Planning a getaway? "Plan a unique day trip around [your local area, e.g., Adelaide Hills] focusing on historical sites and scenic viewpoints," or "Suggest a relaxing weekend getaway for a couple in their 50s, focused on nature and good food." It helps you explore new interests, find new entertainment, and make the most of your downtime.

4.3 Real-World Problem Solving: AI for Life's Little Challenges

Beyond simply boosting productivity and creativity, AI can become a remarkably practical helper for navigating many of life's everyday dilemmas. It can provide different perspectives, help you structure your thoughts, and even draft delicate messages when facing minor challenges or tricky situations.

Drafting Difficult Communications: Breaking Down Tough Conversations. Sometimes you need to write a sensitive email, prepare for a challenging conversation, or respond to a tricky comment. Finding the right words can be hard, especially when emotions are involved. AI can help you phrase things carefully, ensuring your message is clear, polite, and achieves its goal. Ask: "Draft a script for a polite but firm conversation with a neighbour about their dog barking late at night, focusing on solutions and maintaining good relations," or "Help me write a concise and kind email to an old friend explaining why I can't attend their event." It helps you find the right tone and words when you might otherwise feel stuck or overwhelmed by the situation.

Comparative Analysis: Weighing Pros and Cons with AI's Help. When making a decision, big or small, AI can help you lay out the options clearly. It can quickly gather and present information to help you weigh pros and cons, allowing you to see different angles that you might not have considered. Ask: "List the pros and cons of buying an electric car versus a gasoline car, considering cost, environmental impact, and maintenance," or "Compare two popular smart thermostats for ease of use, features, and energy savings." This helps you organise your thoughts and make more informed decisions by getting a structured overview of the situation.

Quick Research & Fact-Finding: Getting Instant Answers (with a caution!). For general knowledge questions or quick explanations, AI can provide immediate answers without you having to click through multiple search results. You can ask: "What is the capital of Australia?" or "Who invented the light bulb and when?" **However, here's**

the crucial caution: Remember, as we'll discuss in much more detail in Chapter 5, it's always wise to **double-check any crucial facts, dates, or highly important information** that AI provides with a reliable, authoritative source. AI can sometimes "hallucinate" (make things up) or provide outdated information. For quick insights or initial understanding, AI's speed is unmatched. But for anything you plan to rely on heavily, a quick verification step is your best friend.

Turning Ideas into Action: Getting Step-by-Step Plans from AI. Do you have a big goal or a complex project but aren't sure how to start or what steps to take? AI can help create a logical roadmap, breaking down daunting tasks into manageable, actionable steps. Ask: "Give me a step-by-step plan to learn how to play the acoustic guitar for a complete beginner, starting with basic chords," or "Outline the key stages and considerations for starting a small online craft store, from product creation to sales." It helps you move from simply having an idea to creating a concrete plan for achieving it.

4.4 Quick Wins: Simple AI Hacks for Immediate Results

You don't need to be an expert to get immediate and powerful value from AI. Here are a few simple "hacks" – clever shortcuts and strategies – to get quick, impactful results right away, making AI an even more seamless part of your daily life.

Leveraging Templates: Reusing Effective Prompts for Consistency. If you discover a prompt that works really well for a specific, recurring task – perhaps drafting a certain type of email, generating a particular style of image for your hobby, or creating a specific kind of list – don't let it disappear! Save it. You can keep a simple note on your phone, in a dedicated document on your computer (like a Word document or Google Doc), or even in a free note-taking app like Notion or Evernote, with your "go-to" prompts. This way, you can simply copy and paste them into your AI tool, tweak a few details, and reuse them instantly. This saves you significant time and ensures consistent, high-quality results every time, eliminating the need to reinvent the wheel for common tasks.

"My Favourite Prompts" Checklist: Your Personal Prompt Library. Take the "template" idea a step further and create your own mini-library of your most effective prompts. Organise them in a way that makes sense to you. You might have sections like: "Work Email Prompts" (e.g., "Draft a professional follow-up email after a meeting"), "Creative Story Prompts" (e.g., "Write a short story about a talking squirrel in a park"), "Image Art Styles" (e.g., "Impressionist painting of a field"), or "Daily Planning Prompts" (e.g., "Create a to-do list for my errands today"). This transforms your AI tool from a general-purpose assistant into a highly personalised, ready-for-action co-pilot, with your most powerful instructions just a click or tap away.

Time-Saving Integrations: Connecting AI to Tools You Already Use (e.g., Google Workspace). While this book focuses on direct interaction with AI tools, it's worth noting that many AI features are increasingly being built directly into popular applications you might already use every day.

Think of your email programs, word processors, or spreadsheet software. Keep an eye out for these built-in AI capabilities. For example, some email clients can suggest replies, or word processors can help you rephrase sentences. These integrations can seamlessly blend AI power into your existing workflow without you having to jump between different websites or copy and paste. They often serve as an "easy button" for accessing AI's capabilities right where you're already working, making your digital life even smoother.

You've just completed a truly transformative chapter, delving into the incredibly practical side of AI! We've moved beyond the "how-to" of crafting prompts and stepped firmly into the "what-for" of daily use. You've seen firsthand how AI can be an incredibly powerful and versatile ally in **supercharging your productivity**, tackling everything from quick email drafts and efficient document summaries to managing your daily plans with ease. You also explored how it can **ignite your creativity**, providing endless ideas for hobbies, crafts, and personal projects, and even helping you learn new things in a personalised way. Furthermore, we looked at how AI can assist in **real-world problem-solving**, from drafting tricky communications to breaking down complex decisions into manageable steps.

A crucial point highlighted for all these practical uses, especially when quickly gathering information, is that while AI is incredibly fast at providing insights, it's essential to exercise a little caution and discernment. Think of your AI as a brilliant, lightning-fast assistant who sometimes gets a detail wrong or misses a nuance. For quick ideas, brainstorming, or generating initial drafts, its speed and capability are unmatched. But for any **crucial facts, important decisions, or information you plan to rely on heavily for accuracy**, always take a moment to **double-check it** with a trusted, verifiable source. This balanced approach allows you to appreciate AI's efficiency for initial insights, while always ensuring the reliability of critical information.

The key takeaway from this chapter is profound: AI isn't some distant, complicated technology reserved for tech gurus. It's a remarkably accessible and versatile tool that can be easily integrated into countless aspects of your everyday life right now. By applying these simple, practical strategies and using the "quick wins" we discussed, you're not just experimenting with AI – you're actively transforming how you get things done, sparking new ideas, and navigating your digital world with greater ease, confidence, and efficiency. You're truly ready to make AI your indispensable everyday co-pilot, enhancing nearly every facet of your life.

Chapter Summary

Chapter 4: AI as Your Everyday Co-Pilot – Practical Applications

- You explored how AI can significantly **boost your personal productivity**, helping with tasks like drafting emails, summarising documents, and organising plans.

- You discovered how AI can **ignite your creativity**, overcoming creative blocks for hobbies, generating unique images, and supporting personalised learning.

- You learned how AI can assist in **real-world problem-solving**, from drafting difficult communications to conducting comparative analysis and creating step-by-step action plans.

- You gained insights into "quick wins" using AI, along with the crucial understanding of when to **double-check important facts** for accuracy.

Chapter 5: Navigating AI Safely & Confidently – Trust, Privacy, & Support

You're well on your way to becoming a confident AI user, creating amazing text and images with your newfound prompting skills! But as with any powerful tool that connects to the digital world, it's absolutely essential to understand how to use it safely, wisely, and responsibly. This chapter is all about giving you the crucial knowledge and practical strategies to navigate the AI landscape with genuine confidence and peace of mind. We'll explore how to tell what's real and what's not in AI's responses, how to protect your personal information, where to find reliable help when you need it, and how to stay informed about AI's rapid changes without feeling completely overwhelmed. Think of this as your essential guide to becoming a savvy, secure, and smart AI explorer.

5.1 The "Truth" About AI: Understanding Hallucinations & Bias

AI is incredibly smart, capable of processing vast amounts of information and generating human-like responses or complex images. However, it's vital to remember that it's a tool, not a human, and certainly not infallible. Sometimes, it can surprise you by making things up or showing an unintentional slant in its responses. Understanding why this happens helps you use AI more responsibly and critically.

Why AI Can Make Mistakes: A Simple Explanation of "Hallucinations." AI models learn from vast amounts of information (data) found on the internet. When you ask them a question, they try to predict the most plausible response based on patterns they've learned from that data. However, sometimes when they don't have a clear, definitive answer in their training data, or when the information they learned was ambiguous or contradictory, they can "hallucinate." This means they generate facts, details, or even entire narratives that sound utterly convincing but are completely untrue or made up. It's not intentional deception; it's more like a very confident guess gone wrong, based on statistical probabilities rather than genuine understanding. For image generators, this can manifest as strange distortions, extra limbs, or objects that defy physics but look plausible at first glance.

The "Always Verify" Rule: Simple Strategies to Fact-Check AI Output. Because of the possibility of hallucinations, it's absolutely crucial to adopt the "Always Verify" rule, especially for any important information. If you're using AI for facts, dates, names, medical advice, financial guidance, legal information, or any critical detail that you plan to rely on, you *must* double-check it with a reliable, authoritative source. Simple verification strategies include doing a quick Google search on the specific fact (e.g., "capital of Australia"), checking a reputable news site, consulting an academic institution's website, or referring to an official government website. For images, if accuracy is key (e.g., is this a real photo of a historical event?), compare it to real-world references from trusted sources. This small step protects you from inadvertently spreading misinformation or making decisions based on incorrect data.

Recognising Bias: How AI Can Reflect Societal Prejudices (and How to Spot It). AI learns from the enormous datasets it's trained on. Unfortunately, much of the data available online reflects the biases, stereotypes, and inequalities that exist in the real world. This means AI can sometimes generate text or images that unintentionally show unfair preferences, stereotypes, or exclude certain groups. For example, if you ask an AI to generate images of "a successful CEO" and it consistently only produces images of men, that's a bias reflecting historical patterns in leadership, not necessarily a conscious choice by the AI. Being aware of this helps you spot it. If an AI's response seems to favour one group over another, or uses language that feels stereotypical, question it. You can even try to mitigate it by adjusting your prompts ("generate an image of a doctor, ensuring gender diversity and various ethnicities") or by seeking out other sources that offer a more balanced perspective. Critical awareness is your best defence against unintended bias.

5.2 Safeguarding Your Information: Privacy in the AI Era

One of the biggest and most legitimate concerns for many people when using AI tools is privacy. When you're typing questions into an AI chatbot or sending prompts to an image generator, where does that information go? Who sees it, and how is it used?

The Golden Rule: Never Input Sensitive Personal or Confidential Data. This is the most important piece of advice regarding privacy: **Do NOT, under any circumstances, type or paste anything into a public AI chatbot or image generator that you wouldn't want shared publicly on the internet.** This includes highly sensitive information like your social security number, bank account details, credit card numbers, passwords, private health information, confidential business secrets, proprietary ideas, or personal contact lists. Public AI tools are designed to learn and improve from user interactions. This means your prompts and the AI's responses are often collected, stored, and might even be reviewed by human trainers to refine the AI's performance. While companies typically anonymise data, the safest approach is to assume your input could potentially become part of their general learning data or, in a worst-case scenario, be exposed in a data breach.

Understanding Data Usage Policies: What AI Companies Do with Your Prompts. Before you start using any AI tool extensively, it's a good habit to quickly look for their "Privacy Policy" or "Terms of Service" (usually linked at the bottom of their website). These documents, while sometimes lengthy, explain how the company collects, uses, and stores your data. Most AI companies state that they use your conversations to improve their models. This means your prompts and the AI's responses might be reviewed by human researchers or used as training data for future, smarter versions of the AI. Some services offer an "opt-out" feature for your data not being used for training, but you usually have to look for it in their settings.

Best Practices for Anonymity: Protecting Your Digital Footprint. If you're brainstorming a personal story, developing a new business idea, or discussing something sensitive, try to keep the details general and avoid naming specific individuals, locations, or confidential facts. For example, instead of: "Write a chapter for my novel about John Smith, who lives at 123 Main Street and works for

XYZ Corp, and his secret plan to escape," try: "Write a chapter for a novel about a character named John, living in a quiet suburban town, and his secret plan to escape a difficult situation." The less specific personal or confidential detail you provide, the better. This simple practice significantly reduces any privacy risks and helps you maintain control over your digital footprint.

5.3 When You Get Stuck: Finding Help & Troubleshooting

Even with all the fantastic tips and tricks in this book, there will inevitably be times when you get confused, when a prompt doesn't work, or when your AI doesn't do exactly what you expect. It happens to everyone, from absolute beginners to advanced users! Knowing where to turn for help and how to approach troubleshooting makes all the difference in staying confident and productive.

Your First Line of Defence: FAQs, Guides, and In-App Help. Before you panic, remember that most reputable AI tools invest heavily in user support. They have excellent "Frequently Asked Questions" (FAQs) sections, detailed online help guides, and sometimes even built-in tutorials or pop-up tips within the application itself. These resources are often the fastest and most direct way to get answers to common problems, understand specific features, or learn how to use a particular command. Don't be afraid to click around, explore the "Help" or "Support" sections, and use their search bars to find answers.

Navigating Online Communities: How to Ask for Help Effectively. Beyond official support, there are huge, thriving communities of AI users online, especially on platforms like Reddit (look for subreddits like r/ChatGPT, r/Midjourney, r/promptengineering), Discord servers dedicated to specific AI tools, or Facebook groups. These can be amazing places to learn from others and get specific advice. When asking for help in these communities, remember to be clear and provide enough detail: Describe your problem clearly (e.g., "My Midjourney image isn't showing any people, only landscapes."), mention the specific AI tool you're using (e.g., "I'm using the free version of DALL-E."), and include the exact prompt you tried (e.g., "My prompt was: '/imagine an ancient forest with magical creatures'."). If possible, include the result you got (e.g., describe it or even share a screenshot if it's not sensitive). This makes it much easier for others to understand your issue and offer relevant advice.

Knowing When to Walk Away: Recognising AI's Current Limitations. Sometimes, despite your best efforts and all the prompting techniques, AI simply isn't the right tool for a particular task *yet*. It's important to recognise its current limitations. For example, highly sensitive, emotionally nuanced conversations (like therapy), truly groundbreaking, unique creative works (where human originality is paramount), or tasks requiring real-time, physical interaction with the world (like driving a car without a human in control today) are still outside the scope of current public AI tools. Don't force AI where it doesn't fit. Recognising its boundaries is part of becoming a truly smart and effective user. It allows you to appreciate its strengths without getting frustrated by its current weaknesses.

5.4 Taming the Information Flood: Staying Current Without Overwhelm

The world of AI is moving at lightning speed. New tools are launched, existing ones are updated, and new capabilities emerge almost daily. While this constant innovation is exciting, it can also feel like trying to drink from a fire hose – overwhelming and difficult to keep up with. How do you stay updated without feeling completely swamped?

Curating Your News Feed: Choosing Reliable AI Information Sources. Instead of trying to read everything that pops up about AI, be selective. Find a few trusted sources that consistently explain AI news, trends, and new features in a simple, clear, and unbiased way. Look for reputable technology blogs, newsletters (many AI companies have their own official ones), or established news outlets that offer balanced and understandable information specifically for a general audience. Unsubscribe from sources that use too much jargon or sensationalise every new development. Quality over quantity is key here.

Focused Learning: Concentrating on What Matters Most to You. You absolutely do not need to learn every new AI tool or feature the moment it's released. That's a recipe for burnout! Instead, focus your learning efforts. Concentrate on the AI tools you use most often (like your chosen chatbot or image generator) and pay attention to the updates or new features that directly help with *your specific goals* – whether that's improving your productivity, enhancing your creative projects, or solving your real-world problems. Give yourself permission to explore other tools or more advanced features only when you feel ready and when they genuinely align with your evolving interests and needs.

Embracing Change as Opportunity: How to Adapt to New Features. Instead of seeing every new AI update as just something else you *have* to learn, try to shift your perspective and see it as a new opportunity. A new feature might make a task you already do even easier, faster, or open up a completely new creative possibility you hadn't imagined. Approach these updates with a sense of curiosity and playfulness, knowing that you'll gradually master them just like you've mastered the basics in this book. Every update is a chance to expand your AI capabilities, not a new challenge to overcome.

You've just completed a truly vital chapter in your AI journey! We've tackled some of the most common and significant questions about using AI wisely and confidently. You now understand that while AI is an incredibly powerful assistant, it's not infallible; you've learned to recognise the potential for **hallucinations** (when AI makes things up) and **bias**(when it shows unintentional favouritism), and crucially, you've gained practical strategies for **verifying information** to ensure accuracy. We also covered the paramount importance of safeguarding your **privacy and data security**, emphasising the "never share sensitive info" rule and helping you understand how your prompts are typically used by AI companies.

Beyond caution, you also gained essential practical skills for **troubleshooting** when your AI doesn't cooperate. No more feeling helpless when a prompt goes awry! You're now equipped with a simple checklist to pinpoint what might have gone wrong, and effective, non-technical strategies like the "one change at a time" method to efficiently fix your prompts. Perhaps one of the cleverest tricks you learned is the ability to ask the AI itself for help when you're stuck, turning it into your personal debugging assistant. Finally, we discussed actionable strategies for **taming the overwhelming flood of new AI information**, encouraging you to choose reliable sources and focus your learning on what truly matters to your individual goals and interests.

With these comprehensive insights, you're not just a passive AI user anymore; you're a discerning and proactive AI explorer. You're equipped to navigate the exciting, ever-evolving world of artificial intelligence safely, with true confidence, and with a clear understanding of its capabilities and limitations.

Chapter Summary

Chapter 5: Navigating AI Safely & Confidently – Trust, Privacy, & Support

- You learned about **AI's limitations**, specifically understanding "hallucinations" (when AI makes things up) and how it can reflect biases, emphasising the "Always Verify" rule for critical information.

- You grasped the essential practices for **safeguarding your privacy**, understanding the absolute rule of never inputting sensitive or confidential data into public AI tools.

- You now know **where to find help and troubleshoot** when you encounter issues, whether through official FAQs, guides, or supportive online communities.

- You developed strategies for **staying informed about AI's rapid advancements** in a manageable way, choosing reliable sources and focusing on what matters most to you.

Chapter 6: AI at Work & Play – Drawing the Line Between Personal & Professional Use

You've learned how to harness AI for your daily tasks and creative pursuits, and you've gained confidence in navigating its safety aspects. That's a huge achievement! Now, let's explore a topic that often brings up questions and can feel a bit complex: how AI fits into the different parts of your life, especially when it comes to work. It's about understanding when AI is a helpful, low-stakes tool for your personal hobbies or everyday errands, and when it requires a bit more thought, caution, and perhaps a check of company policies in a professional setting. Think of this chapter as your guide to using AI smartly and ethically, whether you're relaxing at home or tackling tasks in the office.

6.1 AI in Your Professional Life: Enhancing Your Workflow

Just as AI can boost your personal productivity and creativity, it can be an incredibly powerful asset in your professional life. It's not about replacing your hard-earned expertise or unique skills; rather, it's about giving you a valuable assistant to streamline routine tasks, spark new ideas, and perhaps even help you approach problems from different angles. This allows you to focus more of your energy on the truly important, strategic, and human-centric aspects of your job.

Boosting Productivity: From Drafting Reports to Presentation Outlines. Imagine needing to quickly write a concise summary for an upcoming meeting, draft a basic initial report, or even create a structured outline for an important presentation. AI chatbots can handle these tasks with remarkable speed, giving you a solid starting point that saves you precious time. You can ask: "Draft a concise summary of last month's sales figures for a management update, highlighting key trends," or "Create an outline for a presentation on effective team communication strategies, including an introduction, three main points, and a conclusion." This frees you up from the initial drafting burden, allowing you to dedicate more time to deeper analysis, critical review, and strategic thinking – the areas where your human expertise truly shines.

Creative Brainstorming: New Ideas for Marketing, Projects, or Problem-Solving. Sometimes, in a professional setting, you need a fresh perspective or a burst of new ideas for a work project, a marketing campaign, or solving a persistent problem. AI can be a fantastic, tireless brainstorming partner, offering diverse suggestions that you can then filter and develop. You can use it to generate ideas for a new marketing slogan, explore potential solutions to a recurring operational challenge, or even help you structure a new project plan from scratch. For example: "Brainstorm 10 innovative and cost-effective ways to promote a new software service to small businesses in the local area," or "Suggest creative solutions for improving team collaboration in a hybrid work environment." It can kickstart your thinking and provide a wide array of options quickly.

Streamlining Communication: Crafting Professional Emails and Messages. Crafting professional emails, internal memos, or even customer responses can be time-consuming, especially when you need to be precise, polite, and persuasive. AI can help you find just the right words, maintain a consistent tone, and ensure your message is clear and impactful. Ask: "Write a professional email to a client providing a weekly project update, emphasising key achievements and next steps for the upcoming week," or "Draft an internal memo announcing a new company policy regarding remote work, using clear and empathetic language." This ensures your professional communications are always polished, articulate, and effective, reflecting well on you and your organisation.

Ethical Considerations for Work: Company Policies and Best Practices. This is a crucial point: Before you begin using any public AI tool (like ChatGPT or Midjourney) for tasks related to your job, it is absolutely essential to **check if your company has any specific guidelines or policies regarding AI use.** Many organisations are rapidly developing these policies. Some companies might have strict rules about what types of information you can input (e.g., no confidential data, ever) or how AI-generated content can be used (e.g., must be fully reviewed and attributed). Being aware of and meticulously following these company policies is a fundamental part of being a responsible and ethical professional user of AI. If you're unsure, ask your manager or IT department.

6.2 Understanding Data, IP, and Confidentiality in the Workplace

This is arguably the most critical area where the line between personal and professional AI use becomes very, very clear. While AI can be a fun and helpful personal tool, when it comes to your work, you need to be extraordinarily cautious about sensitive information, intellectual property, and data privacy.

The Absolute Rule: Never Input Confidential Business Information. This cannot be stressed enough: **Do NOT, under any circumstances, type or paste any confidential company data, trade secrets, sensitive client information, proprietary business strategies, unreleased product designs, or internal financial figures into public AI tools like ChatGPT or Midjourney.** As we discussed in Chapter 5, these public tools are designed to learn and improve from user interactions. This means your prompts and the AI's responses might be collected, stored, and potentially used to train future versions of the AI. If you input confidential data, you risk that data becoming part of their general knowledge base, or worse, inadvertently being seen by other users or exposed in a data breach. If your company has specific, private, or internally hosted AI tools, those might operate under different security protocols, but for general public-facing AI, always assume your input is *not* confidential.

Intellectual Property: Who Owns AI-Generated Content at Work? If you use AI to help draft a marketing slogan, develop a report, create a design concept, or even write code for your job, who legally owns that creation? This is a complex legal area that is still actively being debated and defined around the world. Generally, in most professional settings, any work created as part of your employment, even with AI assistance, is considered "work for hire" and belongs to your employer. However, the originality and ownership of AI-generated content (especially if it resembles existing works or is generated without human input) are ongoing legal discussions. For your purposes, always adhere to your company's existing policies on intellectual property and acknowledge AI as a tool, not the sole creator.

Transparency in the Office: Disclosing AI Use to Colleagues and Clients. In many professional settings, it is rapidly becoming a best practice to be transparent about when you've used AI to assist with a task. You don't necessarily need to announce every single AI-generated sentence or image if it's a minor part of your process (like correcting grammar). However, for significant pieces of content, reports, analyses, or creative work that you present to colleagues, management, or clients, mentioning that AI was used as a "tool for drafting," "for initial brainstorming," or "for generating illustrative concepts" can build crucial trust and avoid misunderstandings. This transparency is particularly important for client-facing work, official documents, or anything where the "human hand" behind the work is expected. It's about being honest and setting realistic expectations about the AI's role in your process.

6.3 The Ethics of AI: Being a Responsible User in All Contexts

Using AI responsibly isn't just about avoiding legal troubles or following company rules; it's about being a good digital citizen and understanding your broader impact. These ethical considerations apply whether you're using AI for your personal hobbies, for academic pursuits, or for professional projects.

Avoiding Bias: Recognising and Mitigating Unfair AI Outputs. As we touched on in Chapter 5, AI can sometimes reflect and even amplify biases that exist in the vast amounts of data it was trained on. This means it might unintentionally produce text or images that are stereotypical, unfair, discriminatory, or incomplete in their representation. Always review AI output critically with an eye for fairness. If you notice bias (e.g., an AI-generated list of "top scientists" is overwhelmingly male, or a chatbot gives overly simplistic or biased answers about certain demographics), you have a responsibility to address it. You can try adjusting your prompts to encourage diversity and fairness ("generate an image of a leader, ensuring gender diversity and various ethnicities") or by seeking out other sources that offer a more balanced perspective. Your human judgement is essential here.

Plagiarism and Originality: Ensuring Your Work Remains Your Own. While AI can generate incredibly human-like text or unique images, it doesn't "understand" concepts like plagiarism or originality in the way humans do. It simply draws from patterns in its training data. If you copy and paste large sections of AI-generated content directly, without editing, verifying, or adding your own insights and unique voice, it could be considered plagiarism, especially in academic, journalistic, or professional creative contexts. Always use AI as an *assistant* to your original thought and effort, not a replacement for it. Your role is to inject your unique perspective, refine the output, and ensure it aligns with your intentions and values. The goal is for the final work to be *yours*, enhanced by AI, not simply an AI output.

The "Human Touch" Principle: AI as a Tool, Not a Replacement for Thought. Remember, AI is a tool. It is an incredibly powerful one, but it fundamentally lacks human judgement, true empathy, self-awareness, and original critical thinking. For tasks that truly require deep human connection, ethical reasoning, highly original creative expression, or complex strategic decision-making with a nuanced understanding of human values, AI should *assist*, not take over. Your unique human capabilities – your empathy, your creativity, your critical thinking, your judgement, and your ability to connect with others – are irreplaceable. AI is there to support and amplify these capabilities, allowing you to focus your human strengths on the most impactful and meaningful aspects of your life and work.

6.4 When to Use AI (and When Not To) in a Professional Context

Making smart, informed decisions about when to integrate AI into your professional workflow is a valuable skill. It's about finding the sweet spot where AI boosts your efficiency and effectiveness without compromising quality, ethics, security, or your professional integrity.

Decision Framework: Is AI Appropriate for This Task? Before you use AI for any work-related task, take a moment to ask yourself a few key questions. This quick mental checklist can guide you. First, does this task involve confidential, proprietary, or highly sensitive information (e.g., client data, unreleased product details, internal financial figures)? If the answer is "yes," then you should proceed with extreme caution, likely avoiding public AI tools entirely. Second, does this task require deep human empathy, nuanced judgment, complex ethical reasoning, or truly original, groundbreaking creative output that only I can provide? If the answer is "yes," AI can assist with drafting or brainstorming, but your human leadership, review, and final decision are paramount. Third, is absolute factual accuracy critical, with no room for error, and does it need to be verified against specific, real-time data? If "yes," AI can provide a quick starting point, but thorough human verification against authoritative sources is essential before use. Finally, is this a repetitive, time-consuming, or data-intensive task that AI can genuinely automate, streamline, or provide initial drafts for, freeing up my time for more strategic work? If the answer is "yes," then AI is likely a great fit and will significantly enhance your productivity.

Identifying High-Value AI Applications in Your Profession. Based on the framework above, look for patterns in your daily work where AI can provide the most leverage. Tasks that are typically excellent candidates for AI assistance include: Initial Drafting (emails, meeting minutes, basic reports, project plans, internal memos); Brainstorming (ideas for marketing campaigns, solutions to operational problems, new product features, creative approaches to challenges); Information Gathering (non-sensitive, such as quick explanations of industry terms, general market trends, competitive overviews from public data); Simple Data Organization (turning raw notes into structured lists, outlines, or basic tables); and Content Generation for Public Use (with review, such as social media captions, blog post ideas, press release drafts, always reviewed and edited by a human).

Setting Boundaries: Knowing When to Rely on Human Expertise Alone. While AI is transformative, there will always be tasks that require your unique human skills and cannot (or should not) be fully delegated to AI. These include: Complex problem-solving that requires intuitive leaps or understanding deeply human motivations; Delicate client negotiations or sensitive interpersonal communication; Highly sensitive HR matters, employee relations, or performance reviews; Strategic decision-making that impacts the core direction or values of an organisation; and anything that requires genuine empathy, active listening, and the ability to build trust and rapport. AI is there to support and amplify your capabilities, not to replace your essential human capabilities, judgement, and connection.

You've just completed a truly insightful chapter, bringing your AI journey to a thoughtful conclusion! We've taken a deep dive into how AI can fit into the bigger picture of your life – both personal and professional. You now understand that while AI is an incredible tool to **enhance your workflow** at work, from drafting reports to sparking new marketing ideas, it's absolutely crucial to do so while keeping **ethical considerations** firmly in mind. We particularly focused on the paramount importance of safeguarding **confidential information** and being mindful of **intellectual property** when using AI for professional tasks, providing you with clear "do's and don'ts" to navigate these complex areas.

Perhaps most crucially, this chapter equipped you with a practical **decision framework** for knowing *when* AI is the right tool to lend a hand, and *when* your unique human expertise, judgement, and personal touch are absolutely irreplaceable. You've learned to identify tasks where AI can streamline your work and free up your time, and equally important, you've learned to recognise situations where reliance on AI could compromise security, ethics, or the very human essence of your work.

By understanding these boundaries, practising transparency, and always applying your critical human judgement, you're not just using AI; you're using it *smartly* and *responsibly*. This balanced approach allows you to leverage AI's immense power for productivity and creativity, while ensuring your professional integrity, personal data, and the invaluable human element remain protected. You are now truly ready to integrate AI confidently and thoughtfully into every facet of your everyday life!

Chapter Summary

Chapter 6: AI at Work & Play – Drawing the Line Between Personal & Professional Use

- You understood how AI can **enhance your professional workflow**, improving productivity, brainstorming, and communication in a work context.

- You gained crucial knowledge about **data security, intellectual property, and confidentiality** when using AI for professional tasks, including the absolute rule against sharing sensitive business information.

- You learned about the **ethics of AI use**, including recognising and mitigating bias, ensuring originality (avoiding plagiarism), and applying the vital "human touch" principle.

- You can now use a **decision framework** to determine when AI is appropriate for work tasks, identifying high-value applications, and knowing when to rely solely on human expertise.

Conclusion: Your Confident Path Forward with AI

Congratulations! You've reached the end of this comprehensive guide, and more importantly, you've taken a significant and empowering leap forward in understanding and using artificial intelligence. Remember those initial feelings of being overwhelmed, unsure where to start, or perhaps even a little intimidated by the rapidly evolving world of AI? We've navigated those hurdles together, step-by-step, and now you have the practical tools, clear understanding, and newfound confidence to use AI effectively and safely in your everyday life, both personally and professionally. This isn't just the end of a book; it's the exciting beginning of a new, more efficient, and more creative chapter in your digital journey.

Recap: What You've Conquered and Mastered

Let's take a moment to reflect on just how far you've come. Think back to where we started in Chapter 1. You might have felt a bit lost about **where to even go** to find AI tools like ChatGPT or Midjourney, or simply how to **log in** and begin. We tackled that head-on, providing you with simple, clear steps to access these powerful digital assistants and even explaining the subtle differences between AI chatbots and traditional search engines. You've successfully taken your first steps into the AI world.

Then came the big one: **speaking AI's language** through effective prompting. In Chapter 2, you learned the fundamental importance of clarity, context, and specifying your desired outcome, transforming vague requests into precise instructions that AI can truly understand. You moved beyond basic commands and discovered how to **fine-tune AI's output** in Chapter 3, refining responses with iterative feedback, making the AI adopt different styles through role-playing, and even **troubleshooting** when things went astray – all without needing any technical jargon. You now know how to guide AI to produce exactly what you envision.

In Chapter 4, we explored the incredible **practical applications** of AI in your daily life. You saw how it can genuinely supercharge your productivity (from drafting emails to summarising documents), ignite your creativity (brainstorming ideas, generating unique images), and help with real-world problems, offering genuine "quick wins" that save you time and effort. Most recently, in Chapter 5, we delved into the crucial topic of **using AI safely and confidently**, understanding the difference between truth and "hallucinations," recognising potential biases, and protecting your privacy. And in Chapter 6, you learned to understand the nuances of **differentiating between personal and professional AI use**, ensuring you apply these tools responsibly and ethically in all contexts. You've truly built a robust and solid foundation for interacting with AI.

The Future is Now: Continuous Learning and Exploration

The world of AI is moving at an astonishing pace, with new tools, features, and capabilities emerging constantly. But here's the reassuring truth: that's okay! You now have the fundamental skills, the essential mindset, and the practical strategies to not only keep up but also to confidently embrace this rapid evolution. Think of AI as a constantly growing and evolving garden: you've learned how to plant the seeds, nurture the first sprouts, and prune for the best growth. The future will undoubtedly bring new types of AI, new ways to interact, and even more sophisticated capabilities. Embrace this continuous learning as an exciting and rewarding part of your personal journey, not a daunting chore. Stay curious, keep experimenting with your newfound skills, and remember that your prompt engineering abilities are adaptable to almost any new AI tool that comes along. Your journey as an AI user is an ongoing adventure of discovery.

Embrace the Power: How AI Can Transform Your Everyday and Professional Life

You now hold the keys to a powerful new set of digital tools. Imagine the precious time you'll save on mundane tasks, the exciting new ideas you'll generate for your hobbies and passions, or the polished and effective communications you can now create with surprising ease. AI isn't here to replace human ingenuity, creativity, or connection; quite the opposite. It's here to powerfully **amplify** them. It can free up your mental energy from routine chores, allowing you more time for deeper thought, genuine connection with others, and dedicating yourself to the activities you truly love and find meaningful. Both in your personal life and, with careful and informed consideration, in your professional endeavours, AI is ready to be your indispensable co-pilot, helping you achieve more, create more, and live more.

Your Journey Continues: Next Steps for Growth and Mastery

This book has given you a strong, practical starting point, equipping you with the confidence to dive into the world of AI. But remember, your AI adventure has just begun, and the real learning often happens through doing! Here are some next steps to continue your growth and mastery:

Keep Practising Consistently: The more you use AI, the more intuitive and natural it will become. Make it a habit! Try a new prompt every day, even for small, fun tasks. Experiment with different styles, tones, and complexities. Consistent practice will solidify your skills and unlock new insights.

Join a Community of Learners: You are not alone on this journey. Look for online groups, forums, or communities (like specific Facebook groups, Reddit subreddits focused on AI for beginners, or Discord servers for particular AI tools) where people share their experiences, tips, and challenges. Share your successes, learn from others' questions, and don't be afraid to ask for help when you're stuck. Learning with others can be incredibly motivating and enlightening.

Experiment with New Tools (Gradually!): Once you feel truly comfortable with ChatGPT or Midjourney, allow yourself to explore other AI tools that were mentioned briefly in this book, or new ones that catch your eye. Remember the "focused learning" strategy from Chapter 5 – pick one new tool or feature at a time, and give yourself space to learn it. The underlying principles of good prompting will apply to most of them, making the transition much smoother.

Stay Informed (Wisely!): As the AI landscape continues to evolve, make it a point to stay informed. However, remember to do so wisely, without getting overwhelmed. Follow a few trusted AI news sources, subscribe to a couple of reputable newsletters that explain developments in simple, clear language, and avoid the sensational headlines. Focus on updates that are relevant to the tools you use and the goals you have.

You've truly transformed from an AI-curious beginner to a confident everyday creator. You've conquered the initial setup, mastered the art of prompting, learned to refine AI's output, and understood how to use these tools responsibly across your life. You are now equipped to leverage AI's immense capabilities, not just for productivity and creativity, but to navigate the digital world with greater confidence and enthusiasm. Go forth and create! Your journey with AI has truly just begun, and the possibilities are boundless.

About the Author

Sebastian Huelswitt's journey into the world of complex systems began in Toronto, Canada, and led him across the Atlantic to Ireland, where he completed his schooling and graduated as a Chemical Engineer from the University of Dublin. His passion for optimising processes and managing intricate projects then took him to the University of Aberdeen, where he earned a Master of Science in Project Management. For years, Sebastian has applied this deep expertise in leading roles across global Pharmaceutical and Medical Device companies, primarily focusing on bringing efficiency and innovation to operations and engineering. Today, he enjoys the warm, beach lifestyle in Adelaide, Australia, proving that even with a background in complex fields, simplicity and balance can be found in everyday life.

Made in the USA
Monee, IL
17 September 2026

63414364R00049